In Pursuit of Eve

To Aiva,

Thank You.

Brian Clark

Brian Clark

In Pursuit of Eve
A Sonnet Sequence for Performance

Amber Lane Press

All rights whatsoever in this play are strictly reserved and application for
performance should be made before rehearsals begin to:
Judy Daish Associates Ltd,
2 St Charles Place,
London W10 6EG

No performance may be given unless a licence has been obtained.

First published in 2001 by
Amber Lane Press Ltd,
Church Street, Charlbury, Oxford OX7 3PR
Telephone: 01608 810024

Printed and bound in Great Britain by
Parchment (Oxford) Ltd, Crescent Road, Oxford OX4 2PB

ISBN 1 872868 31 2

For Cherry
with love

In Pursuit of Eve was first presented on Tuesday 20th February 2001 at the King's Head Theatre, Islington, London.

Performed by Brian Clark
Directed by Stephen Clark
Designed by Cathy Wren
Lighting by Charles Balfour
Executive Producer: Ruth Boswell

Author's Note

Sonnet, lyric poem of 14 lines with a formal rhyme scheme, expressing different aspects of a single thought, mood, or feeling, resolved or summed up in the last lines of the poem.

Encarta '95 Encyclopedia.

I started to write this piece as a traditional sonnet sequence following as far as I could the definition above but, even as I was writing it, I became aware that my primary impulse is as a playwright rather than a lyric poet. Yet this conflict within me seemed productive. There is a tension between the narrative drive necessary for the dramatic story and the lyricism that has become, over the seven hundred years of the form, the mark of the sonnet. And this tension is integral, I came to believe, to the strength of the piece.

However, even after deciding to finish the piece as a play for the theatre, the rehearsal process revealed the mixed impulses of its origin. The rehearsal period started with ninety-one sonnets; it ended with seventy-one. Ten of those discarded I decided did not work for one reason or another in either version but there remained ten that, while they had to be cut because they were impeding the dramatic thrust of the story or because we needed to keep the play within an acceptable time frame, nevertheless would work for a reader as opposed to a member of an audience. I have therefore included them in this book but I have asterisked them for two reasons. Firstly, it may be fun for readers to work out for themselves whether or not we were too timid and secondly, I don't want future performers to go through the pain of learning sonnets only to have to unlearn them!

Finally, it is interesting that the sonnet probably started as the stanza form of Italian folk song and as any lyricist knows the best songs in musical theatre are those that carry the story forward as well as dealing with the thoughts and emotions of a character. So perhaps this sequence can be seen as a return to the roots of the form.

Brian Clark, Brighton, 2001

Acknowledgements

I wish to thank my son, Stephen, who encouraged me to write sonnets in the first place, then kept me honest as I wrote them and finally directed the play. He has really earned the sonneteer's highest accolade - he is the "only begetter".

And I wish to thank my wife, Cherry, whose love gave me the subject of this piece.

Part One

1

Earth has many things to show more fair
Than these dull souls at a book launch party.
Critics, writers, would-be literati
Write with borrowed plumes their words in air,
Strutting and fretting and having to blare
Their stolen phrases so stale and hearty
To competing wits and complete shits, arty
Emptiness, stolen from the huckster's fair.
But in this whirling maelstrom I can see
A tranquil centre. A woman – seductively dressed
In silk that traces the curve of a perfect breast.
Petite yet strong, a lively face, free
Of pretence. In this storm, a steadfast quay
In whose sheltered lee I long to be.

2

I wonder yet again what are the spells
A woman casts to draw me to her net?
She is unaware that I exist and yet
I feel her pull in all my tingling cells.
The swelling of that breast? The egg that dwells
Within that womb? Though we have never met,
Her very stance, her being serves to whet
The edge of my desire. Every fibre yells
To move to her. Each pulsing beat compels
My mind to focus on one need: to let
Myself loose in her (though I plan to get
Release without the need for wedding bells).
Nature, nurture, culture all combine
To render me a cypher until I make her mine.

3

Across the room I catch her eye at last
For just a fleeting glance and that is all.
Her eyes go back to a man, so blond and tall
I fear I have no chance, my moment's past.
Yet still I send, with all the strength I own,
My urgent thoughts to make her look once more –
This time to hold the look and pass the door
Behind my eyes to where I wait alone.
That glance again! With eyebrows slightly raised
And lips that tweak into a knowing smile,
Acknowledging my homage without guile,
The practised smile of a woman often praised.
I catch my breath, my blood begins to race.
The smile's the signal. Now begins the chase.

4

The Gods are kind. The Viking has to go,
(His longboat must be waiting at the door).
I watch him leave then quickly cross the floor
To offer her my hand and name and show
The hopeful kind of face that's keen but kind,
A stance that's close enough to indicate
Her charm, but carefully not too close to state
A lack of respect for her peace of mind.
I learn her name, Eve, from Dundee;
Discover her job, a writer (of course),
Say so am I then she's full of remorse,
Damn it! It would help if she'd heard of me!
She follows the rules; she's clearly played before –
This ancient game where only a pair can score.

5 *

My awareness of the room begins to fade
As her gentle smile takes over my sense.
My masculine strength, 'gainst a feminine raid
Stands revealed as a petty pretence.
As always I wonder just how it's done,
These quiet invasions, these soft conquests;
We brag and we say the lady is won
And she just smiles as we beat our breasts.
Our frontal assaults are undermined
With a sapper's skill, an engineer's grace.
They dig a tunnel of which we are blind
Till we fall in love and flat on our face.
But they usually treat their prisoners well
And prison camp can be fun for a spell.

6

Life began in the sea, in primordial soup
With inanimate compounds floating free
(Not unlike this room with its lifeless group
Of people boring to the utmost degree).
Then thunder and lightning, a bolt from the blue
Fused two of those hitherto lifeless specks;
The first protein was made and life ensued,
Later easier (and jollier) with sex!
Our own *coup de foudre* fuses Eve and me.
Our helix doubled, our atoms entwined,
The only sentient life in that dead sea,
Inorganic particles left behind,
We crawl out of the sea onto the sand
Into a public house there on . . . the Strand.

7 *

Away from the weeds, which did provide
Some protection from focused attention,
A certain reserve, a feeling of tension
Between Eve and me, makes us tongue-tied.
We study the menu but can't seem to decide.
To eat or not, that is the question,
I joke and immediately hate the selection
Of yet another quote. So undignified!
I'm becoming disturbed; it's difficult to hide
Increasing unease, a growing apprehension.
Is this a mistake? Better contention
Than forced politeness, boredom inside.
Suddenly she smiles, a melting look.
My fears forgotten, I'm back on the hook!

8 *

The eyes may be the mirror of the soul,
But . . . its doorway is the open smile,
Signalling to other souls there's no hostile
Intent, allaying fears, suggesting a whole
World of possibility. It invites approach
But does not force it, displaying readiness
To respond without demand, indicating steadiness
Of will to accept, without the need to encroach
On freedom. Eve's smile has all that substance
Yet there is more. There is a certain tweak
At the corner of her mouth that is allied
With a glint in her eye that marks intelligence –
Making her smile not anonymous but unique
Open, aware, confident and dignified.

9

As someone said, the course of true love never . . .
She hurries her drink; she has another date!
I am upset but fear to sever forever
The connection with her so I'll have to wait.
Pretending nonchalance I casually ask
If she has any evening free when we
Could see a film or show. I try to mask
My fear of a rival who could vanquish me.
I look nervously out of the window fearing to see
A Viking longboat rowing up the street.
Dammit! Is *he* my rival; it *could* be he
But part of her charm is that she is so discreet.
I will not ask although I long to know
But fake indifference as she prepares to go.

10

She gives me her number; I promise to phone;
I notice that she does not ask for mine.
I look into her eyes and long for a sign
The attraction engendered is not mine alone.
She looks at her watch. How time has flown!
She picks up her bag and finishing her wine
Stands, ready to go. I fail to divine
From her face whether my chances are blown.
We walk to the door then out to the street.
I wish I'd my car to offer a lift
To discover where she plans to go.
I'm sure it's the Viking she's arranged to meet!
And I'm to be carelessly cast adrift
Marooned on a passing ice-floe.

11 *

I strive to think of something to hold her there,
Some urgent question or original clever *mot,*
An elegant crafted sentence to let her know
How very much I'm feeling, how much I care.
But nothing occurs to me; I've lost my flair
For words, my mind a complete blank, a no-go
Area for constructive thought, and so
I merely parade (falsely) a confident air.
She leaves me with a smile and walks away
Across Trafalgar Square, her sinuous walk
Arousing thoughts I'd rather have in bed.
I wonder where's she's going, what she'll say
To him (if him it be) about our talk,
Or if I'm forgotten already. That's what I dread.

12

"Hi Tim, just thought I'd ring for a chat . . .
This afternoon at Charlie's place
I met the most fantastic woman. Ace!
Wham bam! Just like that
I'm head over heels in love . . . Yes
I know I've said that all before
But this time I'm absolutely sure . . .
Maybe . . . middle thirties I guess . . .
No you're wrong, I want to change,
To settle down, stop playing around
And now I'm sure I've really found
The one . . .You'll see. I'll arrange
A dinner . . . as soon as I
Can . . . Love to Helen, Bye."

13 *

The merest possibility will do
As a peg to hang my fantasies on.
A glance, an accidental touch can cue
An innocent affaire or a dangerous liaison
Played out in my mind, enjoyed at length
Unhampered by the constraints of truth
Or likelihood or limits of strength –
Fantasy land is eternal youth.
But there's a limit how long it can run.
The fantasy needs fuel if it's not to fade
It can't keep alive, sustain the fun
If she stays out of sight, no contact made.
A fantasy affaire is all very well –
For a monk, poor sod, alone in a cell.

14

We're made like a jigsaw, with many puzzling parts.
And over our lives we're committed laboriously to try
To make the picture whole – with many false starts,
And we earnestly long to complete it before we die.
Over the years we learn it's impossible to do
With only the pieces provided at the start.
There are gaps, huge holes and no edges too,
Just links to the bigger scene of which we're a part.
Others' jigsaws have parts that fit our own
And parts of ours will find a home in theirs.
We come to acknowledge when we're sadly alone
The smallest group for coherence at all, is pairs.
But finally, the complete picture will only be seen
When a part of each fits every other's scene.

15

I wait two days to phone to make a date
Resolved to keep my cool and make it short,
Better to be understated than overwrought.
"I suggest we see the Turners at the Tate."
She agrees at once; my hopes begin to rise,
"So why not lunch before, we'd keep it light,
We wouldn't want drowsiness to dull our eyes
Or blunt our appetite for dinner that night."
She laughs and agrees to lunch but gently suggests
In the evening she may have to go to see her mother.
She's careful, holding some excuse or other
In reserve to cope with importunate pests.
I agree at once; to show a graceful retreat
Achieves a great deal more than impetuous heat.

16

There are many people within this adult man.
The child who makes demands and screams his need,
The boy, a member of a gang he longs to lead,
Impatient with girls, an ardent football fan.
The adolescent hormone-driven lad,
Racked by urges he finds hard to control,
Face covered in pimples, legs like a foal,
Often excited but more often sad.
The young man who thought his future carefully planned,
The world his precious oyster to open at will
Until the knife slipped due to lack of skill
And there was no pearl, just a bloody hand.
This restless colony where disorder is routine
Seeks peace and unity under a sovereign queen.

17

My heart's in my mouth as I wait on the steps of the Tate.
A balmy relaxing day with the sun on the Thames
Glinting, making the wavelets sparkling gems.
Foolishly I've arrived too early; I dared not be late.
Then on the Embankment I see her golden hair
Shining in the sun, above a short red dress
That caresses her elegant thighs. I have to repress
The urge to run to her; instead I stare
At the river studiously to give me more time
To gather my wits, to become calm and cool –
I don't want to appear an over-eager fool.
Then I hear a quiet "Hello," in her voice sublime.
I turn and look into her smiling face;
My gathered wits disperse to outer space!

18

She offers her cheek, receives my greeting kiss,
A formal gesture, true, but touch enough
To rush my blood; my casualness a bluff
Lest she should hear my heart, divine the bliss
This meeting means to me. For a moment we stand
And look into each other's eyes; I take
Her in, refreshing the image in order to make
Quite sure she's the woman I remember on the Strand.
I quickly check the river, making sure
No longboat has arrived. I take her hand.
She smiles at me, and seeming to understand
My nervousness, indicates me through the door.
Once more I marvel at that feminine grace
Enabling woman from behind to set the pace!

19

But first we go to lunch – in the restaurant of the Tate,
Enwrapped by Rex Whistler's extraordinary mural.
A party journeys happily through whimsical rural
Scenes of hunting and fishing. "It's very appropriate,"
I say, "to bring you here because this painting's called
'In Pursuit of Rare Meats'." She laughs and asks, "And why
Is that appropriate? Unless you think I'm like the deer I
See running, escaping the hunter's gun?" I am appalled.
"Oh no! You're a dear, it's true and it's meet we meet but not
You meet your death, become actual meat! I'm not a barbarian
I don't want to see you on a slab. I'm almost vegetarian!"
God! I hate this tortuous image! Am I a writer or what?
Unless you remember this maxim you're bound to come off worst
The best spontaneous wit is most carefully rehearsed . . .

20

He seems to paint with tinted steam, said Constable
Of Turner, so evanescent and airy. We stand
In awe before the work of genius unfathomable,
Bathed in the Romantic glow from the Master's hand.
The forms of buildings, artefacts, even of man
Dissolve and shimmer in the vibrant swirling light.
The snow, the clouds, the storms, the gales that fan
The fires and raise the seas reveal the might
Of Nature's force untrimmed. I stand with Eve
And feel that force, portrayed before my eyes,
Rise within myself and I perceive,
As I look at Eve, my self as a Turner sunrise.
Art helps us understand what we feel
By making even the intangible real.

21

We leave the Turners, eyes awash with light
And move to the Sculpture Hall, to find some forms
With a harder edge, away from Turner's storms,
To Rodin's 'Kiss'. I smile at the lovers, quite
Controlled in their tender chaste embrace,
Expressing their love without passion which
When not in love I might dismiss as kitsch
But now seems imbued with ineffable grace.
The Redons and Chagalls whose opalescent dreams
Revive the soul; Degas' paintings dance;
Renoir's girls have a rosy, cheeky glance;
Matisse's patterns fly, my whole self teems
With love, but this floor – it feels so bloody hard,
As if designed to punish by the Marquis de Sade!

22

So back to Mr Whistler's room in pursuit
Of rest. The finest display of modern art
Providing no match for tea and apple tart.
The benefit of Art is certainly beyond dispute
But only with time to reflect on what we've seen –
Especially with a sympathetic soul.
We talk of art, of emotion, I feel the goal
I've had, since first I saw her standing serene
In that pretentious mob, is close, then bang!
The thunderbolt! She cannot stay to dine.
Her mother is very ill; a dinner must wait.
She's very sorry. Although I feel a pang
Of anger, I see she needs a genuine sign
Of warmth. So, smiling, "Let's go. You mustn't be late."

23

Victorian stations, cathedrals built for steam,
Like all cathedrals, put us in our place.
We're small and feel, in such vast space,
Our total insignificance in the scheme
Of things. We cling to parting friends to show
How we will hold them in our minds when they
Have gone away. Over and over we pray
Please write! Please phone! So clearly they will know
We need their love and hope that they need ours.
The vaulted glass-roofed space makes us aware
Of our fragility, our transience; it's hard to bear;
We feel the need for help from higher powers.
Our feelings, vented like the steam of yore,
Pervade the sacred space from roof to floor.

24

Though we're not lovers yet (I'm sad to say),
Enough has passed between us since we met
For us to know, with neither leading the way,
A journey has begun, that we are set
Upon a course that leads us who knows where?
Eve does not know how long she'll be away
But I tell her not to worry, I'll be there
When she returns, however long her stay.
"And I can't wait," she says with a gentle smile,
And lifts her face to mine for our first kiss,
Soft at first then opening her lips while
Pushing against me in a meaning I can't miss.
Our bodies speak in far more powerful fashion
Than voices, when the text has turned to passion.

25

She climbs aboard the train; it's one of those
Anonymous modern things with sliding doors.
I want a train with windows that open and close
With a leather strap! There should be binding laws
Allowing lovers to kiss, as in *Brief Encounter*,
While the train moves slowly away gathering speed
He moves with it, she struggles to surmount her
Grief. A proper train! That's what I need!
But no, the doors are closed with haughty hiss,
No slam to represent the breaking hearts,
No lowered window for that final kiss,
A postmodern parting that imparts
No emotion and no passion. So cold and clinical
Is there any wonder we've become so cynical.

26

"Hello?" "It's only me. I'm just calling to say
I'm here. That's silly I suppose." "Oh no
It's not. I'm very pleased to hear you, so
How was the journey?" "It seemed a long way."
"It is! Too far. So come back soon. I'm
Missing you. Really." "So am I –
Missing *you* I mean of course." "It's a crime
To go away so soon, to say goodbye
Before we've properly said hello, so please
Do hurry back." "I will as soon as possible
I promise." "How is your mother?" "Not good, she's
Pretty sick." "I'm sorry. It must be horrible."
And so with stilted words, stumbling, weak,
We fail to let our deepest feelings speak.

27

A week away and Eve's become unreal;
Persistent, recurring images in my head
Keep playing insistently over and over; instead
Of seeing Eve as whole, complete, I feel
My image of her fragmenting in my mind.
I have not known her long enough to keep
A coherent idea encompassing her; a deep
Unease begins to affect me as I find
Her slowly fading away. Each day on the phone
I try so hard to keep the bridge intact;
Some concrete projects that we shared would act
As foundation for love, or binding keystone.
But lacking this, the more that time elapses
It can't be long before the bridge collapses.

28

I've been invited out to dinner tonight.
Pretty depressed, I've had too much to drink.
I flirt outrageously – determined not to think
Of Eve – with Sybil, the woman on my right.
Quite attractive in a sexy kind of way,
Good figure, shining hair, the usual tempting bait
Displayed by low-cut dress. In my drunken state
I sense an opportunity to play.
She seems to accept the touch of my knee, so under
The table I place my hand upon her thigh
Expecting her hand to cover mine. But I
Yelp when she stabs it with her fork. A blunder
Indeed! I change the yelp to a cough, needing
To cover my mouth with my hand to lick the bleeding.

29

You'd think I'd learned my lesson, but still the wine
Is charging my loins; I've never felt so randy,
So after the meal in the drawing room with brandy
I chat up Helen, Tim's wife – lucky swine
Not here tonight, he's on a lecture tour
In Europe. Helen and I have often flirted,
Enjoying the game, but so far, always skirted
The problem of whether we would or would not score
If chance occurred. Tonight we know we can.
She hesitates for just a moment when
I offer to share a taxi with her, but then
She smiles her acquiescence to my plan.
A night for candlelight and pillow talks?
Thank God she's not the type to brandish forks.

30

The taxi stops; again she pauses, thinking,
Then inclining her head, she says, "Coffee?"
Within five minutes I'm sitting on her settee
Working out how I will start, while drinking
Another brandy. I move towards her, she
Quickly says, "We shouldn't be doing this."
I take her hand and soothe her with a kiss
Then looking into her eyes I say, "I agree,
It can only be once, because we both love Tim
But there is no harm – if he never finds out.
It's just a time out of life, to remember throughout
Our lives in secret. I promise we won't harm him."
She smiles and nods; the ground rules are agreed;
She's moved not by my words but by her need.

We hurl ourselves at each other. A crude collision
Not connection. We fall from the sofa and crash on
The floor, trying to convince ourselves our decision
Is forced, the result of overwhelming passion
That cannot be denied. My shirt is torn,
Her blouse is gaping wide, her bra at her neck.
Her nails are ripping into my flesh, we scorn
The tenderness that love can mean, at the beck
And call of lust, that's all. I yank her skirt
To her waist, go down on her, she grinds her crotch
To my mouth; every moral fibre is inert
But so's my prick, wine-soft, I'm going to botch
It. But she takes me in her mouth to suck
Me hard, then like two rutting animals, we fuck.

32

I pull away from her, feeling revulsion.
She flicks down her skirt to hide her pudenda,
Reminding me of Updike's *Roger's Version* –
His footnote on that word that should send a
Message. "Neutral plural of gerundive of *pudere*,
Be ashamed." – I am, looking at us, wrecks,
Pushing away the thoughts of betrayal. It's scary;
The restless mind after mere animal sex,
Denied the peace that loving sex can bring
Desperately wants out, but has to find a way
To part, if not with grace, at least the sting
Of rejection has to be avoided, to stay
The pangs of even wider guilt. But I fear
Only an expression of emptiness would be sincere.

33

I'm walking home, full of self-disgust,
Body poisoned with booze, my spirit expended;
My head throbs with pain, my stomach's distended,
A totally wretched man – and that is just.
Helen and Tim are friends, who should command
My trust. And it's not just Tim that I've betrayed
But Helen too; she's not some whore to be laid
Without a thought. I left without a reprimand
From her; she blames herself, as I do me
And that is right but actually I know
It's not just to myself alone I owe
The duty always to act responsibly
But to my friends, to whom I carelessly bring
The oxymoron of a "friendly fling".

34

And what of Eve? The woman I say I love?
Of course, she needn't know while she's away
I took advantage of the chance to play
The field. But how does that put her above
The others? Is she just a square on a board
Of a game of chance? The dice are thrown; I move
Wherever my counter lands, I can prove
My manhood? How sick! Merely an obvious fraud.
I can't deny I wanted Helen, but then
I also yearn to buy a magnificent yacht
To replace the little boat I've already got;
Does that allow me to steal the money when
I see a chance? Am I still the little boy
Who sulks when he's denied another toy?

35

I'm crawling in a cave that's dank and black
With water dripping on me from the roof.
At the mouth of the cave I left my waterproof
And I can't retrieve it, it's too far back.
The roof is sloping down; I feel the weight
Of the mountain above but I know I mustn't stop.
The roof begins to catch my clothes, the top
Of my head is cut, but I don't hesitate
But still push on till I'm completely stuck.
I begin to panic as I feel the stream that flows
Through the cave, rising to my mouth and nose.
No hope! I'm going to drown! Why wait! I duck
Beneath the water. A ringing in my head . . .
Is coming from the phone beside my bed.

36

It's Eve. That voice that means so much to me!
Waiting to hear it, hoping each time the phone
Rings, it will be she; now I'm thrown
Into confusion. Her voice, a guarantee
Of goodness, pierces my conscience. I'm so sick
In my head and heart; I want last night undone.
Why did I do it! Things badly begun
Usually finish worse. I must be quick
To think of something to say or she will guess!
But Eve just laughs and says, "I'll call again;
I thought it would be safe to wait till ten.
The dinner must have been a great success!"
I don't deserve this woman, that is clear.
That she will find this out is what I fear.

I force myself to relive last night's events.
And see a pattern, all too often repeated
After drinking too much, my sex drive, overheated,
Looks for release wherever, nothing prevents
The determined pursuit of anything in a skirt.
The short-term gain, the only thing on my mind,
There's no question of being considerate or kind.
The chase is all; I don't give a damn if she's hurt –
Until the next morning, then I'm sick with remorse.
A big help to her, who's now feeling degraded
As I am myself, clearly knowing I've basely traded
My self-esteem for trivial intercourse.
This isn't new; I've thought it all before,
Dismissed easily for another chance to score.

38

But do I have a chance to change with Eve?
Certainly now I want to make her mine,
Not just her body, but can I honestly believe
That after making love, I'll still entwine
Myself with her, to seek a more complete
Union, to end this ceaseless dingy dance
From one to another? Or will it end in defeat
And not, for me, a genuine advance.
I so much want it, release, to be finally freed
From chemical necessity; in bond to Eve
Not to my prick, with its pathetic need
For constant change. Desperately I want to cleave
To a person not a drive. The way for me
Is to belong. I'll be damned if I want to be free!

39

"Hello, Eve . . . yes, I'm wide awake now,
I'm calling to say I want to come to see
You. I won't get in the way. You can think of me
Merely a support if you need one. I feel somehow
I need to do this, for me as well as you.
I know we've only just met; it's too soon to press
My suit, so to speak. I want firmly to stress
You needn't see me at all. There's nothing due
From you to me. You don't owe me a thing,
But if you need a shoulder, I'll be there.
Don't worry, I'm not about to chance an affaire
Over your mother's sickbed. I promise. Nothing
Is further from my mind . . . I'll catch the next train . . ."
Can sullied pipers learn a new refrain?

40

I see her, standing at the platform gate
Tensely waiting, before she catches sight
Of me. In jeans and simple blouse, her slight
Figure moves me almost to tears. I wait
Anxiously for her to see me, for the first
Reaction, before she can compose her face
For feigned excitement or politeness. I brace
Myself for either, preparing for the worst.
Her eyes light up at once, there's no pretence;
She runs into my arms and clings and sobs.
Surprised but understanding, my heart throbs
With tenderness. From her grief I sense
Her desperation; I hold her while she cries,
Knowing for sure my decision to come was wise.

Over coffee in the buffet Eve tells me of her pain;
Her mother, a widow (Eve's her only child)
Is fighting every inch, will not be reconciled
To her death. The struggle is fierce; again and again
She rallies from what seems the end. There is no hope;
The cancer, invading every cell, will win
By attrition. She's already painfully thin
And cannot eat. There is no possible scope
For further treatment. Then I'm taken by surprise.
Eve nervously says her mother wants to see me.
She's told her that I'm just a friend, that she
Met me only recently. Eve tries to disguise
Her embarrassment. I take her hand, "It's so
Good I arrived in time to meet her. Let's go."

I stand across the bed from Eve and grope
For words. Her mother winces at every breath;
Her body appears to me the racked rope
In the eternal tug-o'-war between life and death,
Stretched beyond endurance, to the point
Where every fibre screams out for relief.
Every breath is agony, every joint
Crackles with pain. It is almost beyond belief
Her spirit's so tenacious it refuses to yield
To Death's entreaty. Eve gives her morphine;
As the drug seeps through her body to shield
Her from the spears of pain, almost serene,
Her face resumes a human form I recognise:
The model for Eve's quirky smile and gentle eyes.

43

She looks at me and moves her hand to show
She wants mine. I sit on the bed and take
Her hand. "My daughter says I'm not to make
Assumptions. You're just good friends that's all, no
More than that." I see the ghost of that smile,
Whose living form lives in Eve. I nod,
"Sadly that's true but I have plans, please God,
To alter that!" "That's good," she says, "I'll
Have a word with Him – soon." She is grinning,
"We'll see what we can do." She falls asleep,
Eve takes her mother's hand and begins to weep;
I take Eve's other hand making a ring
Of love, as if we have the power to quell
All the evil spirits with a primitive spell.

44

I don't know how but she's survived the night;
She's weaker but still lucid when she wakes.
While Eve is resting I sit with her. She takes
My hand again and grips with failing might;
She asks, "Are you a proper man for Eve?"
I think of Helen; I feel I want to cry.
"Not yet," I say. I know I cannot lie
To this woman about to die; I want to receive
Her blessing. She smiles, "I approve of honest doubt."
"I'll make a promise now," I say. "If I
Win her, and by God I'm going to try,
I'll study to deserve her love without
Ceasing." She smiles, "Good luck! I believe
You. I'm tired now and I need to talk to Eve."

45

An hour later, Eve returns, she's dazed.
"It's over," she says, "Fell asleep then stopped
Breathing." We go into the room. She's propped
Against the pillow, eyes half open, glazed.
I move towards her. Eve places her hand on my arm.
"No," she says, "I'll do what has to be done.
You must go now, back to London. It's none
Of your affair." I'm hurt. I ask what harm
I've done. "None," she says. "With her last breath
She told me what you said. I'm glad, I too
Have burgeoning hope, but she urged we start anew,
To learn about each other with life not death."
I look at her mother, feel her love, then at Eve.
I kiss her there, before her mother, and leave.

End of Part One

Part Two

46 *

I went to her mother's funeral, that seemed
Right but that was six weeks ago. Since then
I've talked to Eve on the phone only when
She called me to talk. I've thought and schemed
Of ways "accidentally" to meet but instead
I think it best to leave it to her so each
Time she's called – two or three – my speech
Where I declare my love is left unsaid.
The talk was merely information, light,
Lawyers, selling the house, choosing a stone.
Is it best for us if Eve copes all alone?
Only time will tell if her mother judged it right.
But as each day slowly passes with my life in suspension,
In my soul and body I feel a rising tension.

47 *

Whenever I ponder the nature of attraction
I'm baffled. I fantasise about Eve undressed,
Her legs, her thighs, her belly and her breast;
Lying with her, in my head, she causes a reaction
That's palpable. Forced to take hold of my self to bring
Release. Yet insignificant amounts of flesh
Distinguish her from countless others. The mesh
Of our minds is good, but again that's something
I share with many. Too soon for us to say
Our minds have melded into a unique shape
Wherein to wander privately, a joint inscape.
It's not enough to stop me wanting to stray.
Yet stopped I am and that's what baffles me.
Why do I feel so high? – at my apogee.

48

I should be surprised her train is late?
Yesterday, at last she called with the wonderful news
She's coming back – but I'm holding back. To enthuse
Too much would not appear appropriate.
She's looking pale and strained; I can see
She's not the woman I knew but a child in need
Of comfort. She comes into my arms. I heed
The call to paternity, she's trusting me.
I gently kiss the top of her head as she cries,
She tells me, for the first time since the funeral;
She's totally drained. I will give her all
The time she needs. To rush would be unwise.
I take her home, the first time in her flat
But I don't stay long. I know she's grateful for that.

49

I understand Eve's pain; a few years back
I, too, had watched my mother slowly die
And remember how hard it was to identify
The nagging core of the pain that continued to rack
Long after the keenest sense of loss had faded.
Becoming aware only slowly how the tap-root
Of my being was cut off; after the brute
Fact of death, the spirit, malnourished, jaded,
Has lost its first connection with the past,
Its sense of continuity and origin.
From damaged roots new shoots must forage in
The earth to take a hold, to break the fast.
But time must pass for these new shoots to grow
And much more time for fresh green leaves to show.

50

Eve is coming to dinner; I'm cooking tonight.
I've never had an old-fashioned courtship like this,
Moving together, kiss by chaste kiss,
Treating her like a maiden and I a knight
In shining armour, strong and brave and courtly.
I have already sallied forth to kill
The dragon – to Sainsbury's – and with Merlin's skill
Transformed him into a roasted chicken and shortly
The trials of fire and water, at my behest,
Will produce the roast potatoes and runner beans,
The gravy, bread sauce, summer pudding that means
My journey's over; I have achieved my quest
And can offer my lady – I'm triumphant, a winner –
The Holy Grail – well, a chicken dinner.

51

The food is passable – just – but the dinner is great.
At first light-hearted, we joke and laugh a lot,
Particularly about the cream which I forgot
To buy, and the beans which deserved a better fate:
Cooked *al dente* – for someone with no teeth.
But the wine is good and the pudding, even without
The cream is excellent. Eve, without a doubt,
Is more relaxed – emerging from her grief.
She thanks me for my tact. I've given her time
To come to terms not only with the loss
Of her mother; six months ago she had been left
By her lover, a bolt from the blue. She'd had to climb
Out of profound depression, the whole of her cosmos
Shattered. She'd felt alone, betrayed, bereft.

52

The dinner's over. In flickering candlelight,
The atmosphere relaxed, I'm feeling sure . . .
The doorbell rings. At this time of night
Who can it be? It's Helen standing at the door.
Looking distressed, she walks straight in. "Tim knows
About us! A bloody nosy neighbour's told him."
Then sees Eve. "Oh God, I'm sorry to bulldoze
In like this." Helen's embarrassed, Eve is looking grim.
And I am standing dithering between the two.
"I'm sorry," Helen says again, "I know
I shouldn't have come." Eve moves to the door. "You
Two have evidently much to discuss, so
I'll leave you now. It's late." Her look's a lance;
I'm pierced by the bleakness of her final glance.

53

Helen begins to apologise, then breaks into tears.
I hold her while she cries, my mind in turmoil;
How can I have been so selfish as to spoil
The best chance I have had for many years!
Helen holds me tight, with passion, my fears
Are growing that what she wants is to embroil
Me further in this affaire, but I recoil
From the thought; my self-disgust rears
Up within me. I know what I have done
Is wrong, and I'm brimming with bitter regret
That I was so self-centred on that night.
And realise I still am if I cut and run.
She feels my mood, becoming more upset,
"You just used me," she says. And she's right.

54

I confess that I have fallen in love with Eve
But will not leave Helen alone to face
The problem I acknowledge is our disgrace.
I suggest we go to Tim to tell him we've
Committed a terrible sin, ask him to forgive.
He's surprised to see us and at first he shows
The signs of anger I expect but he knows
I know something Helen does not – a furtive
Affaire of his last year that must undermine
His moral outrage. He knows I will not tell
But he's in a weak position. He has to quell
His anger. His wife has crossed the same line.
With pain he forgives but I've lost him as a friend;
Some tears in the fabric of friendship nothing can mend.

55

But sadly, there's no quick fix for the loss of Eve.
To her I must seem just like her former lover,
As I was. But since Dundee – her mother – another
Persona has taken me over, I firmly believe,
For ever. But how can I convince her of that?
Tonight as she left, I clearly saw the pain
That she must have feared ever to endure again.
I'm sure she sees me now as just another rat.
Should I wait or try to see her now?
Now's too late, I'll call her in the morning.
I will plead with her, beg her forgiveness, fling
Myself on her mercy but even so I can't see how
To overcome her pain. For I know that she
Has suffered enough at the hands of a man like me.

56

She will not speak to me, answer the phone.
I hear her voice over and over on her machine
Telling me to leave my name, a screen
I cannot penetrate and I have grown
Increasingly depressed, knowing I am alone
Because I deserve to be. Eve's not being mean,
Seeking to punish, I'm sure. But I'm unclean;
Why should she soil her self with me, a clone
Of every inconstant man, willing to trade
The gold of love that will grow, for the dross
Of lust; the scum that appears on the molten gold
Is skimmed and cast away so the metal is made
Free from impurities. So she's right to toss
Me away, every right to be hard and cold.

57

My Dearest Eve, I am going away for a week.
I am writing because you refuse to answer the phone;
This I accept. I deserve it, of course, but am thrown
Into despair as I need to explain myself and seek
Your understanding. So when the telephone rings
It's safe to respond for seven whole days till Sunday.
At four o'clock then I'll ring again and pray
You'll be kind and answer. Just the thought brings
Fearful hope! Eve, I promise I'll not
Hound you or stalk you so unless you speak
To me then, this is goodbye – I feel so bleak;
I love you Eve. And that is true believe it or not.
I'm posting this letter and catching the train to Brighton
Where I have a boat and I hope my spirits will . . . brighten.

58

I'm sailing single-handed to France for no
Reason at all, except to pass the time
Till Sunday. The sea is working its magic; I'm
Relaxing as I feel the ebb and flow
Of waves and tide. Each day I think of Eve
And all that we could be, for while at sea,
Feeling at one with the forces of Nature, free,
With the water beneath and the wind above, I achieve
A peace I never feel on land, reclaim
An order I've lost. Wrapped in the protecting caul
Of my boat, I return to that womb from which all
Of us came. Even the salinity of our blood is the same.
In seven days when I am born once more
I hope she hears my cry from my native shore.

59

I remember as a boy, sailing a boat on the pond.
How anxiously I awaited its return.
And here I am again – anxious beyond
The point I've ever been. I see a tern
Diving into the sea. It surfaces with a fish;
How simple its needs: to eat, to mate, to rear
Its young. All this I have, but also a wish
For something more, some meaning to appear
In the pattern of my life, something significant, more
Than biological routine – and different in kind.
A meaning not temporal or temporary, able to soar
Above the physical, a governance of the mind.
And if this is what I most ardently desire
What the hell am I doing in this sexual mire?

60 *

It's four o'clock, the phone is in my hand
My fate to be decided at a stroke.
I press each digit, feeling myself choke
With all the words I want to say and
All the excuses I want to make. I pause
Before the final digit. I cannot bear
To press it. I amaze myself by offering a prayer
To a God I've equated for years with Santa Claus.
What price faithless prayer! By this I know
How much this means. Eve answer please!
I promise I will be true, I will seize
Every single chance I am given to show
How much I love you. There. I've pressed it at last.
The phone is ringing now. The die is cast.

61

"Hello Eve? . . . yes it's me . . . yes, to France . . . Thank you
For taking this call. Can I see you soon? . . . Thank God
For that . . . I didn't go ashore . . . .. It isn't odd;
Alone, I could think of how we could start anew . . .
Yes that can wait . . . Tomorrow at eight . . . Till then."
I have another chance! She sounded tearful.
What did I expect? A laughing cheerful
Eve? The main thing is we can start again!
Of course one never can or should pretend
It's possible to wipe away the past
As if it had never been, but we can contrast
What was with what could have been, apprehend
The death that was and the life that is, and learn
To make our way, leaving the wake astern.

62

My heart leaps up when I behold Eve
In a sky-blue dress opening the restaurant door.
I stand, she sees me and across the floor
Our looks entwine. Do I have my reprieve?
I cross to her as she walks to me; we meet.
She offers her hand. I lead her to the table.
I'm lost for words, grinning inanely, barely able
To stop myself cheering, leaping to my feet
And dancing wildly around the room. But first
I have to clear away the debris of my former
Life. Never again to experience the trauma
Of that dreadful night. Eve must know the worst
I've been and the best, with her, I hope to become,
To see pure gold when I skim away the scum.

63

At first she doesn't want to listen but I
Insist. Until I have nothing inside me hidden,
Until I feel that there's nowhere in me forbidden
For her to go, I know we cannot fly
Untrammelled by weighty secrets, dragging guilt.
I tell her of my former preference for one-night
Stands, to avoid commitment, and of the plight
Of several women who, like Eve, had built
Hopes and dreams on me, made of straw.
And hardest of all I tell her of Helen, who
Was the wife of a friend used just for a screw,
The knowledge I exploited to avoid a punch in the jaw.
At the end I tell her I'm full of self-disgust
And she's free to leave me now if leave she must.

64

I will not hound or pester her in any way
But I want her to know because of her I've changed.
And even if after this we become estranged
Because of what I've confessed, I want to stay
True to her ideals and I thank her for that.
But obviously I prefer her to stay, to build
With me a love to last, a life to be filled
With trust and joy and children – and a cat
If she wants one! She's not amused, "It's pleasing
You've told me everything – that I've already guessed,
The casual sex, the infidelities and the rest.
But *have* you changed? Or are you merely appeasing
Me? Even if now you're sincere, how can I know
It'll last? Why should I risk another blow?"

65

"My problem is," she says, "I'm not above
The desire for sex, a virgin waiting to bestow
My jewel upon some suitable dashing beau.
In fact I'm a woman in need, a woman in love
With you. If that weren't so, it would be easy
To slip into bed with you to take my pleasure.
It's not that I regard my body as some treasure
To exchange for marriage – that's an idea as sleazy
As anything you've described. I'm not a prude;
I can engage in sex that's just for fun
Or affection; we do have needs and if there's none
To hurt, I see no harm in a permissive attitude.
But not with you. I know myself too well
To embark on a journey leading me to hell."

66

Before I know what's happening she's up and through
The door. I catch her up in the street; she's crying.
"I can't let you go like this," I say, "I'm trying
To tell you I've changed! You've got to believe it's true!
I've been here too often. There has to be a way
To make you see I've changed for good.
Eve, you remember how I said 'I would
Study to deserve your love' to your mother that day.
I knew I'd just betrayed you but didn't lie
When she asked if I was a proper man for you.
And I'm not lying now. Believe me it's true
I love you and beg you to trust me again or I
Am lost even though I know to trust a liar
Is as safe as trusting a pyromaniac with fire."

67

Her crying's stopped, her face an icy mask.
"If you are using the death of my mother to win
Me over and you are not sincere, it's a sin
Beyond redemption. I've only two things to ask:
That you don't play with me. And you wait.
Love, for me, is sacred. For you till now,
Merely a word. For me the word is a vow,
For you, a verbal KY jelly to lubricate
Your way into a woman. You'll not have your way
With me. I want to express my love, but I can't
Until I'm sure. And until then I shan't
Consider you a lover. I want you to stay
To be just friends. If you're prepared to live
With that, OK, but it's only time I'll give."

68

Months have passed and I hope we're growing together.
I find it hard to hold myself in check
And not to offer more than a casual peck
On meeting her or parting. I don't know whether
I'm making much headway, or exactly how
She feels. Doing everything I can to earn
Her trust, laying myself open for her to learn
About me, trying to gauge her feelings now.
We're in a country pub – we've ordered the food.
I'm erect beneath the table. Is that so wrong?
The feelings arising within me are so strong
I want to seize her. No! that's too crude.
Hold her, enfold her, as I hope to in a while.
She sees it in my eyes, responding with a smile.

69

Her hand lies on the table next to mine.
I move my hand; our little fingers brush.
Her smile fades – and with a sudden blush
Her hand responds, our fingers intertwine.
The circuit now complete, the current can flow
From my charged heart to hers and back again,
Warming the blood, enlivening the brain,
Lighting the eyes; I can see hers glow.
The language has changed; mere words have no uses.
The movement back to the maternal sea has begun.
Language there is of tides, the moon, the one
Creative urge that both of us seduces.
We crave the complex deeps beyond the shoals;
The eternal beat is pulsing in our souls.

70

We enter my flat and both instantly recall
The last time we were here, the sudden end
Of growing tenderness. I cannot let a pall
Of sadness, only recently dispelled, descend.
She turns and smiles at me, a little tense;
I take her hand and slowly draw her near;
Our hips and thighs are touching. I can sense
The rising tide of our desire, the sheer
Exhilaration of passion taking control,
Denying the head its customary governing place,
Allowing the yearning heart, the body, the soul
To join with another soul in a passionate embrace.
Her face lifts to mine, my head inclines to her
Our lips meet, and tongues soundlessly confer.

71

The moment when it's clear that she consents
Is charged with swelling joy that's unconfined.
Seduction exploits but spirits intertwined
Act as one; no individual sense
Of taking or giving, just a common need.
I take her hands – there is no need to rush –
And raise them to my lips and gently brush
Between her fingers with my tongue to feed
Both my desire and hers – and it does so –
Mixed with an act of homage offering her
Respect, that I, too, yield and to infer
No sense of conquest, no strutting show.
The rewards of love obey an inverse law:
Ask for less, you will be granted more.

72

We lie upon my bed, still fully dressed,
Enjoying still anticipation's thrill.
I stroke her hair, we smile and talk until
My hand grows impatient and moves to her breast.
She catches her breath as I feel the subtle rise
Of woman's flesh, that holy primal font
That fed at birth and still feeds the want,
The hunger in a man that never dies.
Her blouse slips back, I cup her in my hand
And bend my head and take her in my lips
And while I taste her flesh, I feel her hips
Press against mine as I become manned.
The surge begins within, we feel the urge
To merge, to make our bodies and souls converge.

73

Every single cell that makes up Eve
Contains within its shell an intricate plan
In secret threads, whose task it is to weave
Her unique self – a journey that began
Within another Eve. Each cell is she,
And knowing this I find her every part
Attracts me. Her wrist, her breast, her neck, her knee
Or ankle bone, or ear – wherever I start
To love her, there she is, a life complete.
Except her eggs and here the wonder lies:
They're only half of her. Unless they meet
My incompleted seed, the journey dies.
But if they meet and make our patterns twin,
A new life joining both will then begin.

74

Undressed, I kiss her eyes, then lightly on her lips;
My hand begins to stroke her belly round and round
My little finger climbing every time the mound
Of Venus, brushing through the sacred grove; she grips
My other wrist and lays my hand upon her breast;
I leave her lips and kissing down her neck, I reach
Her nipples standing proud and hard, I give to each
My lips and tongue, and then between them find a nest
To rest my head and feel them on my cheeks. I cease
To move my head, her heart is beating against my face,
Her breath is shorter now; her heart begins to race
As the tension rises towards the inevitable release.
My hand moves down; Eve opens herself to me
And I encounter the moistness of that maternal sea.

75

I leave her breasts to move so slowly down
The ladder of her ribs, that with my tongue
I trace the wave-like form of each sturdy rung.
I reach the temple of her belly and on the crown
The well fashioned by the previous Eve
Where she gave to her daughter at the moment of birth
All the secrets of human life on earth
Wrapped safely in the eggs, ready to conceive.
And they have lain there in their ark for years
Governed by the moon, waiting for each tide
For one to leave the ark, to be a bride,
Then, disappointed, cry her bloody tears.
As I sip at that well I hear that primitive call
That cannot be denied, that holds a man in thrall.

76

My lips now reach the entrance of the temple
And there I plant a kiss in homage due
To that place, that leads to Eve's core, a simple
Kiss, no need to tarry. What must ensue
Is urgently desired by both. Eve takes
My head and draws me up and as I move,
My staff climbs slowly up her thighs and makes
Itself felt where it needs to go then stops to prove
Its willingness to wait till Eve is ready to receive
My love, my need, my seed. Her body says, enter,
The lips are open wide, her hands cleave
To my hips, pulling me into the very centre
Of her being. I am engulfed, feeling her embower
All of my strength masculine with her womanly power.

77

For a moment I pause against her womb, I want to feel her there,
But Nature sternly commands this is no time to serve by waiting,
The turbulent waves of feeling move back and forth mating
My every thrust with hers ensuring that we share
Each tingling thrill in our pulsating course.
Faster and faster we move, not fearing to tax
Our every sinew to reach the climax
Of our pounding desire; we force
Our bodies harder to heave.
Gathered at the root
Ready to shoot
Into Eve.
Press!
Yes!

78 *

New stars are made to shine in the night
Of the cosmic blackness. Particles are drawn
Together by gravity, only by the might
Inherent in themselves. They are born –
From inert matter that never glows –
Of the inexorable attraction of constituent parts.
Drawn together the pressure grows.
Before the star can appear on charts
The pressure has to reach a critical mark
Where fusion can begin, each part will meld
Releasing light into the cosmic dark
As each is joined in unbreakable weld.
We join these stars on this enlightening night,
The world made new by new-star love-light.

79

Still rooted in her earth, her goodness flows
Through my root to every part of my
Whole body and soul. I feel her peace satisfy
My every need for harmony. My soul knows
At last its destiny. I, who have been thrusting
Into her, with all my masculine force
Now feel the greater strength of woman, the source –
And only begetter – of peace. Confidently I am trusting
In that feminine strength of hers as I see her lie
Open and powerfully unresisting on my bed,
To knit those fractious parts of me into one,
That unreconciled, will tear me apart, that defy
Mere will to make them cohere. I here thread
Myself together on the thread by this woman spun.

80

My Darling Eve, this is the second time
I write. I must confess that though I swore
I loved, with love made, I love you more.
I watch you sleep through gentle tears for I'm
So lifted by the honest love we've made.
And I write to make a sacred promise to you.
I swear on the bed where tonight we two
Were joined in flesh and plaited an intricate braid
Of our souls, I will love and care for you for ever,
Not allowing any difference or inevitable strife
To separate us for as long as we both have life.
Whatever else happens to me, I will never
Leave. I sign myself, my exquisite Madam,
Your totally in love, adoring, faithful – Adam.

After the applause . . .

81 – Envoi

There was a reception before the show, the usual clique;
You know, publishers, writers. Not Eve . . .
We were all dressed up, just about to leave
When Jimmy, our second (he was three last week)
Threw up all over her dress – oh what a mess!
She had to stay with him; he was really upset.
And that is how it happens; at the party I met
A woman, intelligent, pretty, funny, I guess
About thirty-eight. She's standing there now. She said
There's a party; she'd like to go but her husband's away.
I've always been faithful; will I really betray
Eve if I go for a drink? But I'll end up in her bed.
The old Adam's not dead; just give him a little scope
And he will rise.
                    But not in me!
                                    I hope!